SHE SHALL BE CALLED WOMAN

Living on Purpose

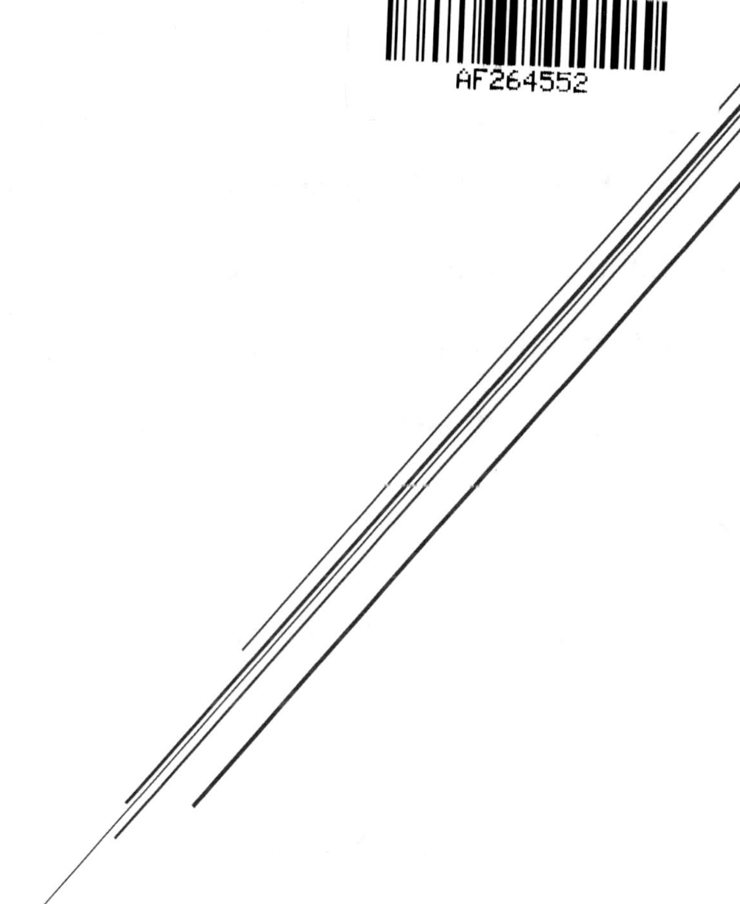

Jennifer Saunders Emedi

Destined for Greatness Publications

She shall be called Woman

Published by Destined for Greatness Publications

Copyright 2014 Jennifer Emedi

Cover Layout by Jennifer Emedi

ISBN 978-0-620-78066-7

Genesis 2:23

She is every Woman

DEDICATION

This booklet is dedicated to every woman who, like me, is authentically living out her purpose and pursuing her destiny.

Maryanne Pale describes her in the following way:

She rejoices in God with a grateful heart and a joyful spirit.

She possesses the ability to genuinely say to another woman: "I admire your qualities and attributes"

She is blessed with the gift of giving and a willingness to help others.

She consoles others even though she too is hurting

She learns from her mistakes and acknowledges that she too is not perfect.

She speaks with words of wisdom and not malice.

From the mouths of destruction, her smile remains unshaken.

She lifts her head and continues to walk in the midst of turmoil.

She inspires other women to be the best they can be

With her life experiences, she touches the lives of a multitude.

She remains determined to be the best person SHE can be

She has the courage to take the fall for another.

She is not too proud to say "I need you"

When her tears fall, she prays faithfully.

When others turn their back on her, she still continues to pray faithfully.

She is humble enough to admit when she is wrong.

Through betrayal and talk, she remains secure in knowing who she is.

She is at peace with herself without having the need to prove herself to anyone.

She values her self-worth and reminds other women of theirs.

She is not pretentious but instead she presents herself just as she is...

BECOMING DESTINY'S CHILD

My Personal Journey

The following pages before introducing this book are a brief look at the beginnings of my personal journey towards understanding my life's purpose and calling.

Let me begin by mentioning that the confidence in my identity which I display today did not come as a specific event but was a gradual revelation through the pages of God's word. I accepted the call to full time ministry during a time when there was much confusion in the body of Christ concerning the role of women in society, politics and the church. Upon entering Bible College, I soon realised that our classes were divided into two groups: pastors and pastor's wives! The pastors as you can imagine, were the men and the girls were prospective wives. We were mostly young unmarried women, called by God, but mostly unsure of how to fulfil that calling without marrying a pastor. The only other option was becoming a highly qualified Sunday School Teacher. Of course there was the option of Missions but that too included marriage at some stage.

Meanwhile, in the secular world, the issue was quite clear cut. The women's liberation movement was in full swing and women were doing it for themselves. Women outside the church were moving forward and finding their place in the world, while in the church, the battle raged on. The main question under discussion being "of what value is the woman in the church?" "Can she amount to anything more than being just someone's wife or mother?"

Sadly, this attitude resulted in the oppression of many women all over the world. I am a product of that era of oppression.

My journey towards liberation began with trying to understand the root of the issues facing women in the Body of Christ and my search led me to the word of God. It seemed to me that from birth, women were actively battling against a force which sought to crush our spirits and destroy our sense of self-worth. I remember the first few months after completing my theological studies. One of the first activities I was asked to join was the local minister's fraternal. That was a nightmare for a young 21 year old woman just stepping into ministry. I had this overwhelming sense of worthlessness. This is really where my identity crisis began but I soon realised that this was Satan's tactic of holding me back from all that God had in store for me. The breakthrough came when I began to see myself from God's point of view instead of man's point of view and THIS changed my life completely.

But before this realisation, like so many other women, I was living under the burden of a lie which was invented by my chief enemy, Satan.

As a young woman in ministry, I thought that the system was my enemy, not realising that I had a bigger enemy who would go to any length to see that I did not fulfil my destiny. His modus operandi has always been the same: look at the stories of Joseph, Moses and even Jesus and every woman since Genesis 3.

In Genesis 3:14-15 we see a disappointed God who still values Eve so much as to declare her the carrier of the deliverer who would crush Satan's head. This immediately places her in a place of superiority over Satan! Of course Satan understood the implications of his curse. He understood the value that God placed not only on Eve, but on every other woman who would be born after her because there was no telling who would be the chosen one. And so the age old war began.

Over the next 4000 years one sees a gradual decrease in the value of women. They even seem to disappear, except for the occasional appearance of a prophetess or judge.

I remember reading the book of Isaiah and understanding Satan's fury when Isaiah began to prophesy: *"Therefore the Lord himself will give you a sign: The virgin will be with child and will give birth to a son, and will call him Immanuel."*

Yet another reminder that God was going to use a woman as a catalyst of his downfall! A woman will carry the weapon that would destroy his works! Wow! The eyes of my understanding were widening as I began to understand the full picture. It was not an organization or denomination that was trying to crush my potential, it was someone who came to kill, steal and destroy.

Operation destroy womankind was in full force until the day when Jesus stood in the synagogue and declared: *"The Spirit of the Lord is on me, because he has anointed me to preach good news to the poor.*
He has sent me to proclaim freedom for the prisoners and recovery of sight for the blind, to release the oppressed, to proclaim the year of the Lord's favor."

This was the day of turnaround, not only for women but for all of mankind. In the book of John we hear Jesus saying: *"The thief came not but to kill, steal and destroy but I have come that you may have life and life abundantly"*

It was then that I realized that Jesus wanted more for me than just breathing. Abundant life meant living God's dream for my life and seeing myself the way he sees me: AS A HIGHLY FAVORED, VALUABLE WOMAN OF WORTH who is destined for greatness and for much more than I can dream, think or desire.

This has since been the defining factor in my life. I pray that it is yours too. I pray that the eyes of your understanding will open to the fact that God has great things in store for you and that your destiny is greater than your circumstances, gender or past.

INTRODUCTION

To introduce this book, we start with some definitions. These are important since nothing is dynamic until it is specific. Definition is important because it brings order and structure to the object of definition. We're living in a season where God is bringing definition especially to the women of the body of Christ. In this season it is God himself who is defining our purpose, it is God himself who is setting things straight and aligning women with his purpose, therefore women are beginning to understand that we're defined by our purpose and not by society, tradition or patriarchal male structures. Our definition as women comes from the purpose of our existence as defined by God and not man or social norms. This is what brings structure and order in my life as a woman. Therefore I submit to you that your journey to understanding your purpose begins with a personal definition of yourself.

We can begin this journey by unpacking the concept of what I call *High Definition Living*. The idea in summary is basically about a life that is defined by its destiny, its purpose or high calling. This idea is built on the understanding that destiny is what gives definition to one's life. There is no life more wasted than one lived without definition. Life without definition is what King Solomon described in Proverbs 29:18 when he said: ***"Where there is no revelation (of destiny) the*** *people cast off restraint"* It's a life without restraint and discipline. Thus we speak of a defining destiny.

Looking at the life of Jesus, who is our ultimate role model, we see how having a clear understanding of his purpose and destiny brought definition to his life and ministry.

This is very evident as we follow his life story from the time of his birth.

It all begins with the angel of The Lord announcing Jesus' birth and with that announcement comes the purpose of his coming into the world. By the time Jesus is born, we understand that he is no ordinary baby boy. We understand through the shepherds, the angels and the wise men that a King is born. But, when we look at the circumstances surrounding his birth, one can easily question his nobility or his promised greatness. You would be forgiven for thinking that the opposite was true and that instead, he was really unfortunate. He was born to an unmarried mom, his father wanted to divorce his mother at the news of the pregnancy, and then to top it all, he was born in a stable. He was born like an outcast. There's nothing great or royal about spending your first few days in a stable.

But that is the exact point of this story. None of these things *defined* Jesus. Neither the stable nor the manger had any bearing on his greatness, his purpose or his destiny.

Whether he was born in a stable with animals or in a five star hotel with celebrities, He was the King of kings. His destiny defined him and those who recognized it came to worship him, because the circumstances surrounding his birth did not change who he was.

HE WAS NOT DEFINED BY THE STABLE, HE WAS DEFINED BY HIS PURPOSE.

His introduction of himself in Luke 4:18 tell us that there was no doubt in Jesus' mind about what he came to do on earth. He said: *"The Spirit of the Lord is on me, because he has anointed me to preach good news to the poor. He has sent me to proclaim freedom for the prisoners and recovery of sight for the blind, to release the oppressed, to proclaim the year of the Lord's favour."*

He repeatedly said; *"I say and do what the Father says"* In John 4 we hear him telling the disciples; *"My meat is to do the will of him who sent me"* In other words, *"My fulfilment is to live the life which the Father has mapped out for me"*

Any person living the life that the Father has mapped out for them is living their purpose. Great people are simply people living their purpose and pursuing their destiny.

It's this destiny which brings definition to one's life.

Jesus lived his life knowing that he was destined for the cross. Because of this, he lived with precision, intention and structure. He had no time to waste chit chatting, hanging around and going nowhere slowly. Understanding his purpose and destiny gave definition to his life.

Definition is an explanation. In other words, your destiny explains the things you do, the friends you keep, the people you visit, the words you speak.

King Solomon said where there is no vision (of destiny) people cast of restraint. This is so true. So true of many women. Not seeing where you are heading can lead one to live a very undisciplined life. One of the main reasons why we as women are not taken seriously is because we do not take ourselves seriously. That means knowing what we are about. What you're about is not about where you come from, the colour of your skin or the texture of your hair. What you're about is what's inside of you. What's inside of you is the seed of purpose and destiny; this seed is the POTENTIAL FOR GREATNESS.

It's really easy to miss the point when you focus on what's outside. It's easy to get distracted and derailed from the main point of your existence. The trick is to understand the investment that God has deposited inside of you, that which is inside of you is the best indicator of the path you should be taking. That which is inside of you is designed to produce greatness. The difference between living a significant life and a great life knowing what's inside of you, knowing why you are here and knowing what you have to offer. Too many of us live reactionary lives because we do not know what we have to offer. We make excuses for our existence and apologize for our presence because we do not understand that our birth announced the arrival of greatness on earth.

Now that you understand those definitions, we can move on to the issue of living on purpose.

LIVING ON PURPOSE

What is living on purpose?

To answer this question, we will start by looking at the word purpose.

Have you ever heard someone say to you, *"you did that on purpose"?* What did they mean? They meant that whatever happened, did not happen by accident, it was done PURPOSEFULLY, OR INTENTIONALLY.

Behind the word purpose is the word REASON. *"There was a reason why you did that"*

Our definition then, can be presented in the following way:

We can say that LIVING ON PURPOSE is really living INTENTIONALLY or living ACCORDING to a plan.

When it comes to purpose in general, we are all familiar with the fact that each one of us lives according to a divine plan.

I think this is the most common use of the word purpose

Much has been said and written about living a purpose driven life and many people were challenged and changed by that teaching.

In this book I would like to take it a step further than our common understanding of being purpose driven.

Let us begin by asking the question: where does our power come from as women?

I want to deal with this question because the answer sets us up to celebrate womanhood.

The answer gives us the understanding that Our POWER comes from our PURPOSE.

A woman who does not understand her purpose is a woman who has been stripped of her power. Too many women have handed over their power to purposeless living, as a result of that, they miss the mark of their destiny because they are not living on purpose.

You see, I believe that Satan was hanging around when God created Adam and then Eve. I believe that as he looked at Eve, he saw her purpose, he saw her power as the giver of life and that is why he bypassed Adam when he wanted to introduce Sin. At that stage Eve had never given birth yet, but her power came from who she was. She was a WOMAN. A woman created on purpose for a purpose. Not created LESSER, WEAKER OR SECOND BEST.

The Old Testament students tell us that creation was a progression of perfection. It was a progression of good, better, best. The cherry on the cake came when God took Eve out of Adam.

Remember what the bible says?

"Then the Lord God said, "It is not good that the man should be alone; I will make him a helper fit for him. But for Adam there was not found a helper fit for him". (Genesis 2:18,20 ESV)

With everything good that God had made, there was still no perfection. There was no completion for Adam and that was an imperfection.

None of the animals were fit to be Adam's helper for the simple reason that his helper, his co ruler and co dominator had to have the ABILITY. None of them were purposed helpers so none of them had the ability designed for that purpose. Their purpose was not rulership but to be ruled.

This shows us that ability is designed for purpose.

The only place where God could find that ability was inside of Adam who was created in the image of God himself.

When God created Adam, he duplicated himself in human form. So when he needed a helper for Adam, someone with

ABILITY, POWER and the POTENTIAL to be a ruler with Adam, it only made sense that this person should come out of Adam because everything that God needed Adam to do was already inside of him. So when God took the woman out of Adam, she was ABLE, SHE WAS POWERFUL AND SHE HAD THE POTENTIAL to be everything God and Adam desired her to be.

Let's just say she was fully loaded!

Fully loaded for her purpose which was only established when Adam saw her. Adam name his wife according to her purpose. Yes, he saw a beautiful woman, but Eve was so much more than that.

SHE SHALL BE CALLED WOMAN

We see this explained in Genesis 2:19

"Now out of the ground the Lord God had formed every beast of the field and every bird of the heavens and brought them to the man to see what he would call them. And whatever the man called every living creature, that was its name. The man gave names to all livestock and to the birds of the heavens and to every beast of the field. But for Adam there was not found a helper fit for him. So the Lord God caused a deep sleep to fall upon the man, and while he slept took one of his ribs and closed up its place with flesh. And the rib that the Lord God had taken from the man he made into a woman and brought her to the man. Then the man said, "This at last is bone of my bones and flesh of my flesh; she shall be called Woman, because she was taken out of Man." (Genesis 2:19-23 ESV)

Adam made this statement in response to what he saw. I believe that Adam had a WOW moment when he saw all the curves. He was in awe of the beauty. When he saw this powerful sexy being standing before him in all her glory, all he could say was WOW!

But what he saw needed a declaration of purpose. What he saw before him was beauty with a purpose and this purpose needed definition by declaration. He needed to name what he saw.

You see, for as long as she was not named, her PURPOSE WAS NOT DEFINED.

We refer to the word for clarity.

"Now out of the ground the Lord God had formed every beast of the field and every bird of the heavens and brought them to the man to see what he would call them. And whatever the man called every living creature, that was its name". (Genesis 2:19 ESV)

In other words, the animals responded to whatever Adam called them. They responded to his God given authority as he named them. Their purpose came alive as Adam spoke their names. **Whatever Adam called them, that was their name.**

Now as we read further, we come closer to a powerful truth which forms the basis of our teaching on womanhood.

"The man gave names to all livestock and to the birds of the heavens and to every beast of the field. But for Adam there was not found a helper fit for him." (Genesis 2:20 ESV)

There's a little powerful word I want us to notice "BUT"

It seems that as Adam was naming the animals, there was a realization that none of them responded to HIS NEED for a helper. None of them were named for rulership, authority or dominion. None of their names spoke of ABILITY. He named all the creatures BUT.....

So God fixed the problem. This is how he did it.

God created a gap in Adam's side to fill a gap in creation. Understand this daughter of destiny; there is nothing inferior about being a woman. There is nothing second rate or lesser, because it takes perfection to create perfection.

 It was that perfection called woman which brought balance, equilibrium and fulfilment to the world.

None of the animals responded to Adam's need because they were not meant to. That was all in God's plan, his plan was to create someone who was able to fulfil her purpose.

And once Adam saw her, he saw this ability. He saw her purpose and he immediately responded to this.

And how does he respond? BY NAMING HER.

"Then the man said, "This at last is bone of my bones and flesh of my flesh; she shall be called Woman, because she was taken out of Man." (Genesis 2:23 ESV)

He did not give her a name, HE CALLED HER WHAT SHE WAS.

A declaration of purpose indeed. When he saw her, he saw more than just a sexual being. He saw more than a beautiful being, HE SAW HIS HELPER.

Of all the females he had already named, as beautiful and as powerful as they all were, none could compare to the one standing in front of him, why?

Because she was like him. She was the female version of him.

How could she be inferior? After all, she was a ruler, just like him. She had authority, just like him. She looked like God, JUST LIKE HIM. So he had no other option than to call her WOMAN or MANNESS.

From then onwards, Eve could live on purpose.

Being "Man ness" meant that she too had a mandate and a mission and she had the ability to accomplish both!

You too have a mandate and a mission. Living on purpose is really your mandated mission. It is doing on purpose what you were designed for. It is really being intentional about living your calling as a woman. It means helping intentionally, influencing intentionally. Ruling intentionally and worshipping intentionally.

This is living on purpose. It is doing purposefully what you were named for.

You were named for authority, named for rulership, named for success and productivity, named for prosperity and fruitfulness.

That's who you are. Woman. Woman of God. Woman of worth. Woman of high regard. Woman living on purpose.

God is calling you to answer to your destiny and purpose. As he calls you, Woman, say yes to all that he created you to be! Say yes to all that you are able to do. Say yes to purposeful and intentional living. After all, it's not for nothing that you are called WOMAN!

POSITIONED FOR PURPOSE

In the previous chapter we saw that God created Eve on purpose for a purpose, which means that when she opened her eyes, she was already POSITIONED for her purpose. We saw that when Adam first laid eyes on her, he named her for her purpose saying **"this one will be called woman"**

In this chapter we focus on the POSITION that Eve found herself in.

In Genesis 2:18-20 we read the following:

"The Lord God said, "It is not good for the man to be alone. I will make a helper suitable for him....

So the man gave names to all the livestock, the birds in the sky and all the wild animals. But for Adam no suitable helper was found."

We're going to focus our attention on that little powerful phrase *"No suitable helper was found"*

We introduced this chapter with the words ON PURPOSE FOR A PURPOSE. Let us now break up the two parts for a better understanding of this truth.

The first part will be ON PURPOSE.

Genesis 1:26 tells us the following:

"Then God said, "Let us make mankind in our image, in our likeness, so that they may rule over the fish in the sea and the birds in the sky, over the livestock and all the wild animals, and over all the creatures that move along the ground." So God created mankind in his own image, in the image of God he created them; male and female he created them. (Genesis 1:26, 27 NIV)

The words "Let us make mankind" tell us of God's intention to create mankind, both male and female.

I need to stress this point because reading Chapter two alone gives one the impression that Eve was an afterthought. Genesis 1 gives us the full picture.

When God saw mankind in his mind and intention, he saw a male and a female. When God saw a ruler of the world, he saw male and female, when God saw a dominator, he saw male and female.

Therefore we can categorically state that Eve was the result of God's purposeful intention.   She did not just fit in, she was God's plan.

She was not created afterwards to fulfil a role or a function, she was there in the beginning as part of God's master plan to duplicate himself in human form.

Genesis 1 explains it so well: ***"So God created mankind in his own image, in the image of God he created them; male and female he created them."***

It was really on purpose, and Eve was part of that purpose.

That is why the bible Genesis 2 says "There was no helper fit for Adam"

This passage is saying that what God had purposed was incomplete. God's plan for his image to be reflected by a man and a woman was incomplete.

And so when God created Eve, he did it on purpose. God's dream was complete when Eve was created. God's plan was fulfilled when Eve was created.

Oh yes, she was a beautiful woman, she was like nothing Adam had ever seen before, but she was more than that, she was God's dream come true!

This is such a powerful truth to me. You see, this is where your value as a woman comes from. Your value comes from the fact that GOD PURPOSED your existence.

YOUR VALUE COMES FROM GOD!

It's not about who you are, who you are not or who you could have been, should have been or would have been if you were born under different circumstances, It's about God.

UNDERSTAND THAT YOU ARE BECAUSE OF SOMETHING GOD DID ON PURPOSE! YOUR EXISTENCE AS A WOMAN IS THE DIRECT RESULT OF GOD'S PURPOSEFUL DECISION!

Which brings us to the second part which is FOR A PURPOSE.

I find that this is where things get a bit fuzzy for women. Because we are so accustomed to taking everything lying down, literally and figuratively, we forget that we have a higher purpose. And sadly, it is in this forgetting that we devalue ourselves so much that we settle for the Devil's scraps instead of God's destiny.

It is in this forgetting that we allow ourselves to wear demeaning and degrading labels, which are not designer labels, they are not labels which are product specific but they are labels which are circumstance inspired.

Devaluing is the result of not understanding your worth as a woman, and that only comes from not understanding the GOD part of your life.

As women we very often reduce our purpose to Adam's need and forget about God's dream.

I would be a heretic if I downplayed the fact that Adam had a real need for human companionship before God created Eve. He had a real need for a HELPER. He had a real need for someone like him. We saw this previously with the naming scenario. But there's so much more to this picture which we often forget and most of our issues as women stem from the fact that we live a one sided purpose. We live as though our existence is purely for man's benefit.

There is too much of God inside of you to be reduced to someone whom God did not design you to be.

There is too much of God inside of you to live a lesser life than God intends for you.

When I think about my purpose GOD should be at the beginning of the questions I ask and GOD should be at the centre of whatever conclusion I come to.

Responding to the name woman is not responding to a sexual inference. Responding to the name woman is actually responding to the high calling of a purpose driven life. It is responding to a God designed and God ordained purpose. It is responding to the God part of me.

Adam said "She shall be called Woman BECAUSE she was taken out of man" Remember why she was taken out of man? In order to create a befitting mate for Adam, God had to look inside of Adam. That's where God's image was. So God took HIMSELF out of Adam to create Eve. When Adam saw Eve, he saw GOD, he saw HIMSELF and he saw PURPOSE and in response to what he saw, he exclaimed "She shall be called Woman."

Remember the need which Adam felt when he was naming animals? That imperfection which God saw when he said "it is not good"? That position was filled by the one who was created for that purpose. She was created on purpose for a purpose.

Daughter of Destiny, if you are not positioned for your purpose, there is something which should be happening which is not happening. There is an imperfection in God's plan until you are positioned for your purpose.

God's dream for Eve was that she would be a HELPER to Adam, for as long as she was positioned next to Adam, she was fulfilling her God given purpose. Being positioned next to Adam placed her in a position of authority and dominion. For as long as she was in God's will, living God's purpose, she was in a position of authority. A God given authority.

There is an authority which God has purposed for you. That authority is linked to your position in relation to God's purposes for you.

Adam could not find fulfilment in any of the animals because they were not destined for ruler ship, but Eve was. So when she opened her eyes, she found herself in a position of ruler ship because it was her purpose to rule.

I submit to you woman of God, that as a woman, your authority comes from your purpose. It is your purpose which places you in a position of superiority and dominion over your environment.

After naming all the animals, Adam could not find one suitable for rulership. When he saw Eve and called her WOMAN, that name set her apart. It set her above all the animals. It positioned her for rulership, dominion and influence. It gave value and distinction to her purpose.

Society, circumstances, ignorance and heritage may have blurred the power and purpose of being called woman but God is presently realigning women to his divine purpose. He is currently repositioning women for purposeful rulership and dominion.

GOD WANTS TO REALIGN AND REPOSITION US FOR PURPOSEFUL RULERSHIP AND DOMINION.

Regrettably, many of us have been derailed from our position of power. Many of us no longer reflect God's image because we have traded in authentic womanhood for something that God does not recognize anymore. This is the time to allow the truth of God's Word to reposition you in line with what God envisioned when he said ***"Let us make man in our own image and likeness."***

WOMAN OF WORTH

As we come to the end of our journey of discovery, we pause for a brief celebration of our value and worth as women but before we can celebrate we need to consolidate our understanding of what it truly means to be a Woman of Worth. We answer the question: what is the WOW factor. This chapter is dedicated to celebrating you, God's woman of worth. The prophetic mandate is to affirm God's value of you. It is to remind you that God has not forgotten you because you are of GREAT WORTH to him!

So what is the WOW factor?

A brief research of the concept yielded the following results:

The WOW factor is a set of properties belonging to an object that pleasantly surprises the watcher.

It is a quality or feature that is extremely impressive.

It is an impressive display brought on by a person or an event.

It is a quality that makes someone feel excited or surprised when they first see something.

Now of course you remember what happened in the Garden of Eden. Here's the exciting thing about that story. Adam is alone, with no suitable helper. It's just him, the animals and the angels. All beautiful beings. All awesome in their own way. All stunning and fantastic. Then GOD CREATES Eve and Adam finally has a WOW moment. Adam opens his eyes after his operation and is pleasantly surprised by God's work of art. He is IMPRESSED by God's handiwork. The quality, the precision and the purpose brought one expression to his lips: WOW!

That was the effect God was going for. As a designer, God was going for the wow effect. Eve was not just another creation, she was a woman of great worth.

Six thousand years later, God still manages the same effect, because that's the effect he was going for when he created YOU and when he looks at you he is extremely impressed by his handiwork. When he looks at you he does not see a failure with a bad track record, he does not see a nobody in somebody's corner. When God looks at you, he sees a woman of great worth, because that's the way he created you. When he created you, he placed great worth and value on your life and that worth is the reason why you are still standing. It's the reason why you keep on going even when the going gets tough, it's the reason why you survive the worst attacks, it's the reason why you win the toughest battles, it's really the reason why the devil can't get rid of you no matter how hard he tries. It's because YOU HAVE THAT WOW FACTOR!

Let's look quickly how the Bible describes a Woman of Worth. To do this of course we go to Proverbs 31. Here the wise king is advising his son about what to look for in a woman. Looking through the entire passage, you will see that Solomon said nothing about outer physical appearance.

If only our young men could understand that outer beauty is neither strength nor courage. That outer beauty does not account for the true worth or value of a woman.

If only our young women could understand that the WOW factor has very little to do with the hips and thighs but has everything to do with what's inside. The true value and worth of a woman is what's inside of her. The treasure within is the treasure of God and it's this treasure which cannot be touched or destroyed.

Yes, it's true, God worked much on the outside but he invested everything on the inside.

Proverbs 31:10, 17, 25 reads:

"A worthy woman who can find? For her price is far above rubies. She girds her loins with strength, and makes strong her arms. Strength and dignity are her clothing; and she laughs at the time to come."

Solomon is speaking about a woman who is worth far more than rubies.

One of the saddest situations is watching young women giving themselves away for nothing. By nothing I'm not talking about money, dowry or token, I'm speaking about NOTHING!!! Giving yourself to someone who has nothing to offer you is a sure indication that you do not understand your worth. It is a sure indication that you do not understand how expensive you are. God has deposited too much of himself into you. Selling yourself short is devaluing yourself. Understand that if you do not value YOURSELF, nobody else will. If you do not see yourself as more precious than rubies, then nobody else will. Understand that all you need to be successful is already inside of you. Everything you need to be impressive and brilliant is already inside of you. You were born as a woman of worth.

Now what makes a woman of worth? Three words come out of our passage: She's a woman of

Strength

She dresses herself with strength and makes her arms strong. (Proverbs 31:17 ESV)

Have you fought some battles which looked above your ability? Have you faced some giants which looked like they would destroy you? You've climbed some mountains which looked like they would drain all your strength. And on top of all that, you held down two and three jobs to make ends meet. And you're still standing. Stronger and better. Your scars are your testimony. Not because of your good looks but because of your strength. YOU, DAUGHTER OF DESTINY, ARE A WOMAN OF WORTH!

Of course there are still many rivers to cross, there are still battles to be won, and God is banking in the fact that you have the WOW factor so you are conditioned to win!

Your strength is not a GOOD thing, it's a GOD thing.

And that is why you are more precious than rubies. Because inside of you is a deposit of supernatural strength which is designed to carry you through every adversity you may face and even when you feel like you're too tired to carry on, your inner strength rises up and cause you to mount up with wings as an eagle. You precious daughter of destiny, are a woman of strength and as God looks at you he says WOW my daughter, you are awesome! You are a celebrity in heaven today, because you have that WOW factor. God is impressed. God is pleased.

Dignity

Strength and dignity are her clothing. (Proverbs 31:25 ESV)

She has the ability to keep it together even when she feels she's losing it! She fights her battles without lifting up her skirt, without raising her voice and without making a scene. She wears dignity like a royal garment.

An awesome quality indeed. It takes a woman of dignity not to stoop down to Satan's level. When somebody said something which did not deserve your response. You refused to stoop to their level and dignify their foolishness with a response. Something out of your control happened and you did not respond as everyone expected. You held your head up high, you kept your mouth shut and you committed the matter to God. You went into your room, closed the door and poured out your heart to God instead of shouting, screaming or panicking. Yes, that's because you are a woman of worth. You have that wow factor which sets you apart and makes you different from those around you.

WOW, it took a lot to keep it together, to keep it neat and tidy, but you did it WOMAN OF WORTH!

<u>**Preparation**</u>

"And she laughs at the time to come." (Proverbs 31:25 ESV)

She doesn't know what the future holds but she knows who holds the future. She is prepared with a testimony in one hand and the Word of God in the other. She can laugh at the days to come.

A woman of worth knows that she looks better in her future than she does in her past. She lives each day purposefully in preparation for her destiny.

So, to answer Solomon's question: ***"A worthy woman who can find?"*** God has found in you a worthy woman. You are worthy of his grace and his favour. You are worthy to be his vessel unto honour. You are worthy to carry the surpassing splendour of his glory in your frail jar of clay. Worthy to be a carrier of his gifts, talents, ability and Presence.

This book celebrates you. Woman of great worth, strength, courage and dignity. A woman who values herself and fights for what she believes in. A woman who won't give up on her dreams regardless of how many obstacles stand in her way.

That makes you beautiful, fabulous and absolutely amazing. Just the way God intended you to be.

DESIGNERS ORIGINAL

We are constantly hearing the following phrase today: ***"You do you and I'll do me"*** For me this is more than just a phrase because I find that there are just too many "Copy Cats" in the church. I find too many people are dissatisfied with who they are and who God called them to be, so instead of focussing on being the best they can be, they are very busy trying to be someone else. This is very sad because if I am not me who is going to be me? If I am not me then the world is missing out on a piece of HEAVEN. If I am not me then GOD is missing an opportunity to be glorified. God is glorified by me living who he designed me to be. God is not embarrassed by me, I am HIS creation. That makes me a DESIGNERS ORIGINAL. So, if you are busy wanting to be me, you're only going to be a cheap fake of a great original.

Believe me, woman of God. You will be much stronger and more effective as soon as you begin to understand that you are here by divine design. Your life will have more meaning as soon as you understand that you are here on purpose, not by mistake, not as an afterthought and definitely not as a second attempt. You are the original version. Never before seen on earth, and never to be seen after you die! This is it. And so when you begin to understand this, you make every second count.   You live on purpose and definitely do not make excuses for your existence, because your existence is intentional and it is DIVINE.

When you begin to learn to celebrate you, you will stop trying to be everybody else. When you learn to celebrate you, your life will be more meaningful. Your ministry will be more effective, and God will be glorified.

Living as a designers original is living with the knowledge that you exist for God's glory. A lot has been written about living on purpose in this book. But what does living on purpose mean to you? It means living THE REASON for your creation. When you understand why you are here you will understand what you must do while you are here. Many women find themselves going nowhere slowly. Why? Not because of the colour of our skin, not because we're previously disadvantaged, not because of our social standing or current circumstances. We are going nowhere slowly because we do not know why we are here. Many of us feel that because our parents did not plan for us, God did not plan for us. No, your life is not meaningless, daughter of destiny, you are here by God's design.

This book is meant to encourage you to celebrate your authentic self. It's time to embrace and love who you are because loves who you are. This book is a celebration of YOU because you were wonderfully and fearfully made.

I like to call you I AM MADE because you were made by the Great I AM.

Now this is a bit of a tongue twister because depending on where you place the emphasis, the meaning changes.

Do you know what is meant when a label says something is "Custom made"? It means made according to specifications. When a label says "handmade" It means made by hand.

YOUR label, daughter of destiny, says I AM Made.

So, on the larger scale of things, none of the other stuff really affects or defines you. Why? Because God used a boy and a girl. He borrowed some sperm and an ovary so that you could be human. He used a set of circumstances so at you can have a history, but all of that is not you. It's the canvas that God used to make you. Which means that there is NOTHING INFERIOR and NOTHING SECOND RATE about you. That makes you more than a NOBODY. It makes you more than a SOMEBODY and definitely more than an ANYBODY.

You are a unique, special, well-made designers original!! You're unnecessarily well made. You wear a divine label, made in heaven! That is why your salvation came from heaven. Your restoration came from heaven. It cost God all he had to get you back, why? Because you are His creation. Your label will never change.

Psalm 139 is the moment you have been waiting for!

"For you created my inmost being; you knit me together in my mother's womb. I praise you because I am fearfully and wonderfully made; your works are wonderful, I know that

full well. My frame was not hidden from you when I was made in the secret place, when I was woven together in the depths of the earth. Your eyes saw my unformed body; all the days ordained for me were written in your book before one of them came to be." (Psalm 139:13-16 NIV)

Psalmist David says "For YOU CREATED Me"

This is where I want us to land this book. I want to bring the message home to every lady reading me. I'd like to put a few things into perspective so that you understand that the concept of a Designers Original is not just a fancy popular idea. It in fact goes to the CORE of who we are.

Hear David as he says: " it is YOU, Jehovah, (Elohim-Creator God) the Great I AM who CREATED me.

Wow. Can you feel the power of this statement? Because if you really can, if you can really feel the creative power of Elohim flowing through you from the crown of your head to the soles of your feet. If you can understand that YOU are here because GOD CHOSE you to be here. If you can understand that there's NOBODY else on earth like you. Then you will understand that you are a LIMITED EDITION. You will understand that you are GODS GIFT TO EARTH. That is why Angels respect you. That is why demons despise you. Because you are not like the rest of creation.

Do you know the difference between you and the rest of creation? On the first five days, God created for PROVISION. On the sixth day, GOD CREATED FOR HIMSELF. Which means that you, precious Woman of God, were created for the Creator. You were created according to the creator's specifications.

When we're introduced to God in Genesis, He is stepping into nothing but his very presence changes the atmosphere and "nothingness" must have understood that ELOHIM the CREATOR had just arrived. And when the creator arrives, anything is possible. And so He speaks and things fall into place. He sets things in order in preparation for his MASTER CREATION. His provision was for his Master Creation, but his master creation. Was for HIM.

That is what God would like you to understand through this book. There is nothing ordinary about you. You were created by a perfect God, for a perfect God. So EVERYTHING about you is perfect.

Well, Jen, what about what about my slightly oversized this and that? What about my this compared to that?

Thank you for asking. I would love to address the issue of comparison. You will never be able to celebrate your authentic self if you want to be someone else.

David says "I will praise you for I am wonderfully made". Which tells me that living an authentic life celebrates the handiwork of God.

Understand that no matter what feels out of place, when God looks at you, he sees Himself. He sees the Great I AM. Which leads me to conclude that you are a quality product. Not cheap quality, not fake quality, but I am quality. God loves what he made, he loves what he sees, he loves who you are, so if you cannot celebrate what you see, at least celebrate what GOD sees. Celebrate what God knows about you and what God sees in you because what He sees in you is bigger than your small body. It's bigger than your big body and it's much bigger than who you think you are not.

And so I end in Psalm 139 again where David says: " I will praise you for your **works** are wonderful"

Are you able to praise God for YOU?

Are you able to look at yourself in the mirror and say: THIS GIRL IS **I AM** MADE! Yes there are scars, yes there is brokenness, maybe even some insecurity but in spite of that my label says I AM made. I was created in HIS image and bought with a price. I'm here on purpose and from today the world is going to know that I AM wonderful, I AM awesome! I AM powerful and I AM a Woman of GOD.

AMEN.

She shall be called Woman

By Jennifer Emedi

SHE SHALL BE CALLED WOMAN

She is God's woman, God's dream, God's design.

Naturally beautiful

Supernaturally powerful

Built on purpose and awesome in design

SHE SHALL BE CALLED WOMAN

Woman of worth, Woman of valour, Woman of strength

Amazing influence

Creative ability

Weak in her physique but unequalled in her strength

SHE SHALL BE CALLED WOMAM

A loving woman, a caring woman a praying woman

Curvaceously unique

Purposefully beautiful

She's a show stopper, designer label woman

I CALL HER MOM. SISTER. DAUGHTER. FRIEND

God calls her woman, for she was brought out of man

Called to destiny

Prepared for purpose

She entered the world in response to God and man

HE CALLS HER HELPER. WIFE. LOVER. DREAM COME TRUE

She shall be called woman, for so she is

Predestined by name

By divine design

She came to earth in answer to who she is

WOMAN.

Jennifer Emedi

DESTINED FOR GREATNESS PUBLICATION AND PROCLAIMATION

For Conferences, Corporates, Seminars, Workshops & Camps

082 074 7988

073 289 2688

jenne@destinedforgreatness.co.za

Founder of African Woman Rising Ministries

Author of:

Unshakeable Faith

Destiny's Child Series

The Masculine Mandate

Facebook: Jennifer Saunders Emedi

Twitter: @jenne201

www.destinedforgreatness.co.za